How to Avoid High Child Support Payments and Not be a Deadbeat Dad

by Gerald Taylor

LETA TR
Arkansas MMXIV

How to Avoid High Child Support Payments and Not be a Deadbeat Dad

LETA TR

P.O. Box 7042

Sherwood, AR 72124, USA

Ordering Information visit www.amazon.com or visit
http://letatrpublishing.com

For regular updates, tips, and advice, subscribe to
http://avoidhighchildsupport.com

Editor: Barb Lauger
ISBN-13: 978-1517004057
ISBN-10: 1517004055

First Edition

Printed in the United States of America

DISCLAIMER: This book and any information contained herein are intended for informational purposes only and should not be construed as legal advice. Seek competent legal counsel for advice on any legal matter.

Contents

Preface

Child support, while good in concept and theory, is a flawed system filled with a wealth of biases. The system dates back to the pre-19th century when groups would come to the aid of poverty-stricken people, including single mothers and children, by providing them with work and paying for their services. Those groups would provide just enough funds to prevent the recipients from utter destitution.

Subsequently, the organizations would attempt to recover paid wages from the receiver's family, specifically fathers. Once acquired, those funds belonged to the groups and were not given to the mothers or individuals receiving assistance.

Fast forward to the 20th century; child support allocation was left to the complete discretion of the presiding judge in the court where the case was decided. However, in many cases this method resulted in major disparities, because there was no specific "formula" used to determine this decision. Consequently, it was extremely complicated for parents paying child support to have input in ongoing attempts to get a fair monthly payment. This, unfortunately, played a big role in non-custodial parents not honoring support payments.

For this reason, the Office of Child Support Enforcement was created in 1975 with the objectives to:

- Search for absent parents
- Establish paternity through relevant evidence
- Determine child support amount availability and enforcement

The CSE proposed that monetary abandonment might be considered criminal conduct. And if a parent avoided payments for more than two years, and the back payments accrued to more than $10,000, a sentence of two years imprisonment in a federal penitentiary could be levied.

And now in the 21st century, child support laws have gotten even more strenuous to enforce payment. Moreover, many times the payments aren't reasonable for the non-custodial parent to satisfy. Court-ordered child support assignments are geared to guarantee the rights of the child and don't put forth much importance on the obligations that you may have (although your responsibilities can be taken into account) to support yourself.

Consequently, non-custodial parents are faced with a downward spiral of actions taken against them, making it almost impossible to recover from. Some of these atrocities can include:

- Warrant(s) issued for arrest and imprisonment

- License(s) suspended and or passport revoked
- Income taxes offset
- Garnished paychecks
- Difficulty finding employment

For the most part, child support laws erroneously postulate to account for the costs of the children within one household. While there are many parents who choose not to financially support their children, there are many who do. Consequently, those parents are required to support two households—their own and that of the custodial parent.

State governments historically have been unwilling to address this common issue, considering they receive federal funding for child support. They also have the added benefit of legal fees that are collected from paying parents who are in various stages of the system, and the receipt of federal funding for each inmate they have in a penal institution.

Therefore, this guide is intended to give parents with unfair and unreasonable child support payments information to establish a balance between contributions on your child's behalf from the state and your own personal savings.

This book's objective is to not only protect the interests of children, but also to prevent destruction of the parent's assets, capital, and livelihood. We will explore methods to determine fair monetary payments and how to set up a system that will force the state to honor those agreements.

When Child Support Payments Exceed What Your Income Can Support

It is more common than not for non-custodial parents to be issued child support allocations that far exceed what they are capable of sustaining. In some cases, joblessness, loss of income, illness, injury, or other circumstances beyond one's control can manifest challenges to meet child support requirements.

If for any reason you aren't able to keep up with your child support obligation, it is your responsibility to request a payment modification with the courts. To do this, contact your local child support office. They can assist you with the complete process. Another option is to file a *motion to modify child support* order—the pleading filed with the court to make changes in the best interest of your child. It is strongly advised that you seek legal advice before filing any motions with the courts. However, if you can't afford a lawyer, take the *Jurisdictionary* course. Having not been able to afford a lawyer myself, who quite frankly probably wouldn't have helped much anyways, I purchased the course and benefitted greatly from it with my own child support case.

The *Jurisdictionary* course includes videos and audio clips that teach you, "How to draft pleadings, write and file motions, make effective courtroom objections, set hearings, get admissible evidence into the record, cross-examine witnesses, and how to prepare your case for appeal in case you lose in the lower court." For ordering information visit: www.howtowinincourt.com?refercode=PL0021.

When you appear for your hearing, it is imperative that you bring proof of your current income. Also, inform the courts of your circumstances—for example, you lost your job—and the steps you're taking to resolve them. However, let me caution you that quitting your job, or having an unexplained or consequential reduction in your income can result in an unfavorable result on your behalf. The judge can refuse to lower your payment, and may instead raise your payment based on what the court believes you are capable of paying.

If you don't have joint custody of your child, ask the courts for more visitation. As previously explained, this can be done by contacting your local child support office for instructions, seeking an attorney, or completing the *Jurisdictionary* course to learn how to file a *motion to modify child custody.*

Having more visitation can allow the judge to adjust the child support amount due to the expenses incurred while the child is with you. If you are currently spending more or equal time with and money on the child than the mother is, this can benefit you in court. Make sure to keep thorough and detailed records of the days that you have the child, and all expenses accrued for those days.

Finally, note that if the child has a job, income, or inheritance that the custodial parent has no access to, this can also be used to justify a lower child support payment or elimination of the obligation altogether. Make sure you have all necessary documented proof to support your request to modify child support.

When You Have Arrears or Past-Due Payments

If you owe arrears or have past-due payments, you can make payment arrangements with the court. To do this contact your local child support office for instructions, seek an attorney, or complete the *Jurisdictionary* course to learn how to file a m*otion to modify child support.* Consequences to refusing to pay the child support balance or simply ignoring the obligation can result in:

- Income tax returns being offset for balances greater than $500 in arrears
- Passport being denied for balances greater than $2,500 arrears. (Note that if you have to work or travel internationally and are on the passport denial list, you may be able to work out

a plan with the court and receive your passport back or be taken off the list.)

Usually after filing, the court will give you a low payment amount for a few years until the arrears or past-due balance is paid off. Also, be aware of your state's statutes of limitations for past-due child support. In some states, after a number of years of non-payment, the past-due payment becomes legally uncollectable. Contact your local child support office for more information on this.

It's best to go to court and make arrangements to pay instead of hiding or running from the obligation. Doing this will only exacerbate your issues.

When Assets and Capital Have Been Affected Because of Past-Due Child Support

Generally, wage withholding is applied in almost all cases where child support arrears is relevant. In addition to wage garnishment, the following methods may be taken by the CSE without a judgment of the court:

- Offsetting of federal and state taxes over $500
- Placing a lien on real estate property and other assets
- Freezing of bank accounts
- Denying passport (if the amount owed is over $2,500)
- Forfeiting dividends from the sale or rental of properties
- Revoking your professional, occupational or recreational licenses

The following are payments that the CSE can't garnish:

- Payments intended specifically for veteran's affairs (excluding early retirement)
- Federal grants for students
- Payments generated by the concept of economic vulnerability (not including unemployment insurance) and retirement payments for employees of the railway system
- Payments for social security,
- Those that are excluded by decision of the federal office billing system are typically immune from child maintenance agreements

Regardless if your payment(s) fall within the realm of the CSE's reach, just note that garnishment can only occur if regular payments are delayed for more than 30 days, or more than $25 in back-orders is owed.

To mitigate any interference with your capital, open a trust and transfer all of it to the trust's accounts. Note that it is imperative that you not perform this action if you're currently in the midst of a seizure by the CSE. There are laws against the fraudulent conveyance of assets in child support cases, and evidence of such may allow the court to seize your trust.

The first step to opening a trust is to obtain a federal tax ID number (EIN – Employee Identification Number) for the purpose of tax administration. You can acquire one online by visiting www.irs.gov.

Once you begin the application process, it is imperative that you open a "revocable" trust. By doing this it allows you to shield your assets from the public. The trustee (someone you trust) manages the trust for the beneficiary—the owner (you). And typically the beneficiary is kept private. An additional benefit of having a revocable trust is that only the recipient of the trust knows the properties that have been registered in it.

After acquiring your EIN, open a bank account using the trust's EIN. This will allow you to protect your money from future seizures. So if you work a regular 9-5, be sure to keep all of your savings in the trust's account. The CSE can only garnish income in your name and social security number, and not that of the trust, since it is a separate entity.

Personally, I recommend starting a new small "business," under the trust's name. A small business can be something as simple as collecting unique shaped potatoes and selling them over the Internet. So this means that the trust and company's name will be something like "Bill's Funky Potato Company."

It doesn't really matter what the business entails. The goal is to be able to take advantage of some of the benefits of starting your own business including, but not limited to:

- Putting all of the "company's" assets into the business' name, including bank accounts, homes, cars, etc. In this case, if legal actions are brought against you, only the belongings in your name can be impacted. Any assets associated with the company cannot be considered.

- Specifying your own income and providing proof of that amount to the courts in order to have your child support reduced.

All assets fully owned by the company should be in the business' name. This includes real estate, even if it is the home that you reside in. Your place of residence can also be the same location as the business, and therefore, it should be under the business' name. Utilities—phone, cable, Internet, etc.—are also inclusive. If the car that you drive is used for the business in any way—for example, going to pick up the funky shaped potatoes—it should be under the business' name. Any investments in physical plant, or equipment—laptops, printers, etc.—should be under the name of the company.

As previously mentioned, you can be an employee of the revocable trust company with a monthly salary allocation and still maintain a regular job. But remember, all money that's associated with your name and social security number, will be used to consider child support payments.

Additionally, you should be sure of the maximum amount allowed in your state for salary withholding, which will also give you an idea about how much can be required to meet your child support obligation.

Tips and Advice

If at all possible, try to negotiate a fair monthly child support payment with the custodial parent. If this isn't an option, seek legal counsel. Of course, not everyone can afford a lawyer, therefore, contact your local child support office for advice. Or, as mentioned, you can also look into taking the _Jurisdictionary_ course, which I assure you is worth the investment.

Keep in mind that the success of a fair allocation for support orders depends largely on your capability to argue and demonstrate how you are actively involved in safeguarding the interests of your child. A judge will never allow your economic interests to prevail over securing a decent standard of living for your child. In the eyes of the courts, the child must have the opportunity to at least have a decent living status for his age, similar to the status of the parent who holds higher income.

Do not be ostentatious, buying expensive cars and homes or taking exotic vacations in your name. This includes posting images on social media of your luxury assets for the purposes of appearing to be successful. The CSE can verify this and justify you having large child support payments because of your lavish lifestyle.

Do not hide your assets or income in a way that the CSE may find them; it has access to large databases to track all of your possible sources of income—including casual prizes and gifts. So it is not a good idea to try to reduce your records of property without good justification, and ultimately these behaviors can be punished with child support payment amounts far greater than the ones you would have met if you cooperated from the beginning.

If you are notified by the court, attend all subpoenas, reconciliations, interviews, lawsuits, and other requirements. Remember that failure to do this can lead to you paying unreasonable child support. It also provides a free access card to investigate all your sources of direct, indirect, and occasional income.

Try to stay informed about the status of your case by contacting the courts and CSE regularly. You could be penalized for not responding to failed notifications. Some notices can be filed without tax classification, which means without you participating. These reasons are enough to affect the amount of your child support contribution.

If you suspect that the custodial parent doesn't want to keep you informed about case developments in order to get a quota which may benefit him/her, you should be calling the courts or CSE weekly to ask about the process. Never forget that you have a moral and legal responsibility to give your child the support he or she deserves for good overall development. Check the laws of your state to have full knowledge of the specific ones that apply to your case.

Do not lose contact with your child; your responsibilities go far beyond the economic ones. Being actively involved in your child's life makes it easier for a judge to consider the expenses you invest in him with more time spent.

If you are required to recognize a child that you have never seen, or are unsure about paternity, insist on a test to check your genetic affiliation with him/her. This can delay the child support process and give you time to prepare your case to win a fair child support order.

On the other hand, if you think that despite your efforts to achieve fair child support payments, they have resulted in giving the custodial parent a means to capitalize for her own benefit, you can always ask for a review of the order. Request for the custodial parent to indicate in front of the CSE or judge how this money will be spent on behalf of your child. In some cases, if that parent can't justify the amount requested, or has unreasonable uses for the money, the judge can make a decision on your behalf.

Keep all available information about your income up to date and orderly, because you will certainly have to provide it to the relevant bodies that calculate your child support fee. Do not attempt to deliberately hide information that may be obtained through third parties and is directly related to you through personal documents. Doing this is basically telling the CSE that you want to pay less even though you're able to pay more.

****

I sincerely anticipate that this book has provided you with the confidence needed to battle the CSE and their unfair rulings. Also, I hope that we've exposed the injustices of court ordered child support and associated laws. Expectantly, non-custodial parents have received efficient resources, tips, and advice to help them "avoid high child support payments."